The Best Disguise

THE BEST DISGUISE

Poems by
Susan McLean

The University of Evansville Press
Evansville, Indiana

The text of this book is composed in Baskerville.
Composition by R.G.
Manufacturing by Thomson-Shore.
Book and Cover Design: W.B. & R.G.

Library of Congress Cataloging-in-Publication Data

McLean, Susan, 1953-
  The best disguise / by Susan McLean. — 1st ed.
    p. cm.
  ISBN-13: 978-0-930982-68-3 (hardcover)
  ISBN-10:0-930982-68-1 (hardcover)
  I. Title.
  PS3613.C5775B47 2009
  811'.6 — dc22   2009034059

Some of the poems in this collection have been published or are forthcoming in
Arion, *The Barefoot Muse*, *Blue Unicorn*, *The Chimaera*, *The Classical Outlook*, *Dust &
Fire*, *Farming Words*, *The Formalist*, *14 by 14*, *Holding Patterns*, *Hunger Mountain*, *Iambs
and Trochees*, *Kiss and Part: Laughing at the End of Romance and Other Entanglements*, *Light
Quarterly*, *Lucid Rhythms*, *The Lyric*, *Measure*, *Mezzo Cammin*, *The National Poetry Review*,
The Neovictorian/Cochlea, *PMS: poemmemoirstory*, *The Raintown Review*, *Schuylkill Valley
Journal of the Arts*, *Slant*, *Sonnets: 150 Contemporary Sonnets*, *SSU Impact*, and *Umbrella*.

The author wishes to thank the McKnight Foundation, the Loft Literary Center,
the Mary Anderson Center for the Arts, and the Southwest Minnesota Arts and
Humanities Council for fellowships and grants that supported the writing and
submission of poems in this book.

The University of Evansville Press
1800 Lincoln Avenue
Evansville, IN 47722
(812) 488-2963

For Philip Dacey and John Finamore
Sine quibus non

CONTENTS

I. *Deep Cover*

II. *Farming the Netherlands*

III. *Like the Boys*

I. *Deep Cover*

Deep Cover

Nakedness is the best disguise.
When you discard the final veil,
it always takes them by surprise.

Because men think that compromise
is weak — that if you yield, you fail —
nakedness is the best disguise.

Though you expose your breasts and thighs,
your mind is as opaque as shale.
It always takes them by surprise

to find out that the body lies.
Surrender can conceal betrayal.
Nakedness is best. Disguise,

equivocation, alibis
can be seen through. To lay a trail
that always takes them by surprise,

hide nothing and you'll blind their eyes.
Go ask Judith. Go ask Jael.
Nakedness is the best disguise.
It always takes them by surprise.

Self-Portrait, Age Ten

After our fifth-grade teacher had us draw
pictures of ourselves, which she displayed
on the wall, I glowed with pleasure when I saw
that mine was nearest the truth. I had conveyed
my sleeveless shirt and pleated skirt, brown eyes
and yellow hair, of course, but best of all,
the parts were roughly of the proper size,
the head and limbs not overlarge nor small.
But when I saw Elizabeth's sketch, I froze,
dismayed. Her head was larger than her body,
with huge blue eyes, a rosebud mouth, no nose,
small feet, and a wasp waist. She looked a beauty
and I looked like a chunky child. I burned,
stung by this vision out of all proportion,
half baby and half Barbie. How had she learned
to draw like that? Could beauty be distortion?
Was it her mom, the hairdresser, who'd taught her?
Mine was a chemist. Fighting off the blues,
I studied the techniques I'd never use —
not lovely but precise, my mother's daughter.

The Limits of Art

Hearing that Pat, my friend of sixteen years,
had a massive tumor the size of a cantaloupe,
over the next two weeks I fought off tears
and tried to scrape together scraps of hope.
Her mother's death from cancer scared us both
as we rode the waves of helplessness and grief.
When her oncologist pronounced the growth
not cancerous, I was legless with relief.

Next day, a brilliant poet in his prime
(greater than Pat or I will ever be)
died of a stroke. His voice, lost for all time,
was passionate, unique. But now I see
where love of verse and love of persons end.
I'd say to Death, "Take Shakespeare. Leave my friend."

Unscripted

This is no fairy tale, no dream come true.
You're awkward when you first meet, unaware
of any sudden spark. It could be you

just want a date and like somebody who
can make you laugh. You're sick of solitaire
and dying for a dance. No dreams come true,

but daily calls are nicer than you knew.
Your parents disapprove, which makes you care
more stubbornly. Later, it could be you

just skip the something borrowed, something blue,
and find a cheap one-bedroom flat to share.
Living on cold cuts is no dream come true.

You learn to cook, to budget, to make do
with chicken livers and *vin ordinaire*.
After you've finished school, it could be you

take jobs in different states, as you pursue
your dreams. Once more, your voices bridge the air,
mile after lonely mile. No dreams come true,
but someone dies at the end. It could be you.

Figs

Because they don't grow this far north; because
when I'm in Italy or France, it's June
or earlier; because my parents raise them,
but when I visit, always it's too soon
or late for that year's crop; because they're sold
in tiny cartons at outrageous cost
and not for long; because they're slippery
and sweet as sin inside, and outside, soft
as breasts; because, once ripe, they split apart,
and rot or wasps destroy their fragile treasure;
because I know I'll never get enough,
I always eat them with a groan of pleasure.

For Brian Schmiesing

July 11, 1951-Dec. 12, 1997

Take care, he always said, leaving.
And I did — I took and took,
a debt I can't repay with grieving.

The setting sun, beyond retrieving,
gilds stubble with one backward look.
Take care, he always said, leaving.

He gave as if he were receiving,
as if he wished he could revoke
the debt I can't repay with grieving.

The newly risen moon this evening
hides her eyes with a rag of smoke.
Take care, he always said — leaving

me here dismayed, still not believing
that he canceled at one stroke
a debt I can't repay with grieving.
Take care, he always said, leaving.

A Woman of a Certain Age

I read more slowly now, because I read
between the lines. The heroes of my youth,
who gave their lives for justice, art, or truth
(consumed with purpose, driven to succeed),
now seem like puppets pulled by strings of need,
while those who died unknown (except by those
they fed, taught, nursed through illness, mended clothes
and cared for) doled out grace unmixed with greed.

A quilt, a tablecloth she hand-crocheted,
some tips for making piecrust, kneading dough,
the memory of a gumdrop tree she made —
small things of use, of beauty, of delight
are what they leave when they have left our sight.
Don't tell me what such gifts are worth. I know.

The Demon Lovers

Even as a teen I should have known
those long-haired boys who sang so well of sin
were mine to see and hear, but not to own.

Every howl of longing, every moan
that made the small hairs prickle on my skin
thrilled me with danger. But I should have known

that nothing crushes like a rolling stone.
The music's over just when you begin
to feel the beat as if it were your own

ecstatic pulse. Together but alone,
taken outside myself and taken in,
I drowned in moonlight. But I should have known

the wild and hungry face that I was shown:
the stranger in the mirror-pool, my twin.
Those boys were lost in mazes of their own —

trapped in a strutting pose they've long outgrown,
imploding from the emptiness within
or dead by twenty-eight. I should have known
that demon loves have demons of their own.

The Wave

For Eric Markusen, 1946-2007

A tropic scene — thatched huts, some clumps of palms,
and people running from a towering wave —
haunted my childhood like the atom bombs
we heard about in school. Nothing could save
those people in the drawing in my book
from the crushing cliff of water. I could swim,
but I'd been swamped by smaller waves. One look
and all hope of surviving it grew dim.

My colleague who researches genocide,
who picks through wreckage looking for an answer
to why the hatred sweeps in like a tide,
has learned he's facing pancreatic cancer.
Now it's his turn for sorrow, courage, fear,
watching the wall of water drawing near.

Vamping

I find that I can imitate Mae West,
learning to run before I even crawl.
The trick is not to say, but to suggest,

that I am knowing, sly, and self-possessed.
The boys who shunned me as a know-it-all
perk up when I can imitate Mae West.

It helps that I already have her chest,
though not, alas, her wit, panache, or gall.
The trick is not to say, but to suggest.

Even my drama teacher is impressed —
he switches me from crones to *femme fatale*
on finding I can imitate Mae West.

She always played her cards close to the vest,
knew when to hold or fold and when to call.
Her trick was not to say, but to suggest,

that though she viewed carnality with zest,
she wasn't anybody's living doll.
I find that I can imitate Mae West.
The trick is not to say, but to suggest.

Transit

I swim above a web of light,
a shadow passing through. The pool
is empty, but for me, and bright.
I swim above a web of light,
delighting like a bird in flight
through blue expanses, deep and cool.
I swim above a web of light,
a shadow passing through the pool.

Dark Shadows

A high-school friend was hooked on the mystique
of vampires, filled with vaguely sexy dread
by Barnabas, who, if he weren't undead,
would look like a forlorn and haggard geek.
She watched his daytime soap five times a week,
voraciously. At nineteen, when she wed,
she decked her windows and the waterbed
in purple-velvet mortuary chic.

But who am I to talk? I had my own
Vlad the Impaler, singing in a band —
I, too, a good girl eager to depart
from goodness, but determined to disown
complicity, pretend I'd never planned
to say "Give me that stake right through my heart."

No Monsters

"Ain't no monsters out tonight" we sang —
then shrieked and ran, as one kid from our gang
would lunge out of the shadows like a shark
and seize another running through the dark.
Even at five, I knew that *ain't* was wrong,
but yelled it out with gusto in our song,
giddy at daring night to do its worst.
But soon our mothers called, and we dispersed
back to our homes and dreams, in which we knew
that monsters did exist. They always do.

For Cathy Cowan

May 16, 1946-Dec. 22, 2001

Because she had so much to share,
she found the way she had to live.
No matter how much time or care
the takers take, the givers give.

Parties, dinners, helping hands —
whatever she could give or make
she did, for strangers and for friends.
The givers give; the takers take.

Her shyness sometimes made her curt
or brusque, which some would not forgive,
and few could tell that she was hurt.
The takers take; the givers give.

She loved to sing in choir, to play
the bells, to laugh, to try to shake
the loneliness and blues away —
but givers give and takers take.

She poured her generosity
like honey draining through a sieve.
Yet in the glow of memory
the takers fade; the givers live.

Reasons

The heart has its reasons that reason cannot fathom.
— Pascal

It isn't simply friendship, though you were
my first and only friend. It's not mere lust —
though when you take your shirt off, you still stir
tremors and aftershocks. It isn't just
because you make me laugh. If that were all,
I should love Woody Allen just as much.
I'm dazzled by your power to enthrall,
but Clinton, too, possessed the common touch.
It's not because you cook and not because
you give my goals the weight you give your own.
It's not just that you overlook my flaws
or that, for my career, you live alone
for nine months out of twelve. It has to be
because — against all reason — you love me.

The Cape

Mired in adolescence, prone to mope
about the solitude I can't escape,
I buy a hooded, floor-length navy cape,
lined with satin, belted with tasseled rope.

It doesn't keep me warm. The wind whips through
the armholes, making it billow like a sail.
No matter. No mere comfort could prevail
on me to give it up, though I turn blue.

I look like some medieval votaress,
I think, an Héloïse or Guinevere,
someone remote in time and place from here,
with some more poignant, glamorous distress

than mine — that I'm excluded and ignored.
I'm not quite here myself. I live in books,
gliding past snide remarks and sidelong looks
and sleepwalking through high school, where I'm bored.

Sheltering, like a turtle, in my shell,
I hope the future's closer than it seems,
for I have no defenses but my dreams
to get me through this season spent in hell.

Alas

"I've never heard that word from anyone
but you," my friend Jan comments with a laugh
while reading the translated epitaph
of some poor Roman, dead at twenty-one.

I know I've merely said it tongue-in-cheek,
implying mild regret and resignation,
not the aching cry of desolation
and suffering too unbearable to speak.

These days, we've lost the language of lament.
We're taught to suck it up or take a pill
when sorrow strikes. We have more days, and still
once they are gone, we don't know where they went,
facing the same disasters without warning
or even a vernacular of mourning.

Unrequited Love

Love is a talent; you can never learn it.
When it rubs your ankles like a cat,
you can reject it, but you can't return it

to its owner. Yell at it or spurn it —
it curls up mutely on your welcome mat.
Love is a talent you can never learn. It

can't be wiped out or created. Burn it,
starve it, devastate its habitat —
you can reject it, but you can't return it

to a state of placid unconcern. It
pays you back with interest, tit for tat.
Love is a talent. You can never learn. It

gives itself to those who cannot earn it.
You may ignore its pleas, presuming that
you can reject it. But you can't. Return it

or not, someday you'll be the one to yearn. It
figures — irony's a democrat.
Love is a talent. You can never learn it.
You can reject it, but you can't return it.

Hemorrhage

For Sandy Fuhr, 1947-2008

First blood is always a shock. When what's inside
pours out, escaping from its bodyguard,
time's tourniquet or bandage is applied
and, mostly, we survive — though paler, scarred,
and never as trusting of that traitor, skin,
whose smug integrity has proved a fraud.
How easily we and it were taken in,
then learned its flimsy barrier was flawed.

At first we tell ourselves that time will heal
our map of cuts and gashes. Then once more
life's edges rip a hole nothing can seal;
the red stream runs; we're emptied, as before,
of what the heart needs most. The blood flows on
till everyone we care about is gone.

Feral

She'd left her heart open, just one small door,
enough to let a shivering pet get warm
on icy nights. But in dashed a fanged horror
and crouched in a corner, hissing. With a broom
she tried to shoo it out. It showed its teeth
and snarled, its beady eyes red-rimmed and dire
as it slashed and worried at a squirming truth,
exposing scars she'd never meant to bare:

A group of girls, age nine. A whispered lie.
Some coins that — it was rumored — one girl stole.
A post of trust she lost at the school store.
The teacher who wouldn't look her in the eye
or fondly call her pet names anymore.
A blast of wind. A heart with a hinged hole.

For John

Here in this little room we rest, still glowing
from exertion in the drawn shades' gloom,
naked, content, not caring what we're showing
   here in this little room.

A breeze billows the shades; the faint perfume
of lilacs washes in, then ebbs, time slowing,
mired in honey, till its steps resume.

Yet even as we pause, I'm overthrowing
the tranquil privacy that you assume,
betraying you to different kinds of knowing
   here in this little room.

Small Funeral

For Dr. Grant E. Hess, Jr., 1913-2007

The last great-uncle dies, the baby of
his family, still lagging far behind
the others, stripped of everything but love:
his wife, his golf, his liberty, his mind.
The church is nearly empty. Had he died
soon after he retired, there would have been
crowds of his friends and patients. There abide
only his offspring and a few close kin.

Graveside, young men in uniform attest
bureaucracy's long memory. With gun,
bugle, and flag they convoy him to rest,
one last debt settled. And when we are gone,
would we prefer the same oblivion
to dying while our spouse and friends live on?

Prime Movers

Because when no one talked to me, Keats crooned
a soothing song and Byron made me laugh.
Because notes set me dancing, but words tuned
my heartstrings. Because meaning is just half
their pull. Because they hiss and stomp and sigh
and meet, like parted lovers, in a rhyme.
Because the mermaids sang my lullaby
and warned me there's not world enough and time.
Because I shaped a figure and it breathed.
Because I once was silenced by a sneer
for nineteen years. Because the silence seethed
like proofing yeast. Because I always hear
the pulse of breakers in my inland sea.
Because free verse was too constrained for me.

Like Bede's Sparrow

Like Bede's sparrow
(or was it a swallow?)
I flash through a narrow
hole into a hollow
hall, only to arrow
back out, where none follow.

The light at the heart
of the mystery, cast
by warm love or cool art,
in a moment has passed
from the dark at the start
to the dark at the last.

II. *Farming the Netherlands*

Doors

Death is a fickle lover. He was curt
when I came knocking on my father's grave —
not even a small crack opened in the dirt.
I rattled the locks on every door: the cave
of the crawl space under the house; the jar of pills
gleaming in darkness, like a pile of skulls;
the scarlet door of the razor in my skin;
the cold blue door of the water in the bay.
Galloping through furrowed fields, I'd pray
the lips of earth would open and let me in.
But the pills would not stay down; the gashes healed;
the water bore me up, as water does.
Weary at finding every exit sealed,
I opened the oven door, and there he was.

A Little Horaceplay

Gather rosebuds while you may;
drink your fill of Cabernet.
     Joy is wasted
     if untasted:
seize the doughnut — and the day.

See the world, but see it slant,
dancing till you reel and pant.
     Never measure
     wine or pleasure.
Water's fine — if you're a plant.

At my back I always hear
Death unhooking my brassiere.
     Love comes late
     to those who wait —
grab the boy and chug the beer.

Tip a pint or down a quart;
play your favorite contact sport.
     Put the action
     in attraction —
death is long and life is short.

Music, laughter, wine, and thou
(all the bliss the heavens allow) —
     though tomorrow
     bring us sorrow,
Paradise is here and now.

Gatekeepers

They've never been inside themselves — the critics
who bar the gate with rules and dare the writers
to jump it — but they know exactly who
got in before and that you're not like them.
They watch you narrowly, shaking their heads,
exchanging witty quips and knowing smiles,
prepared to wait forever. But the ones
inside call out that the gate is always open
and that they never jumped for anyone.
They sent themselves in a letter to the world,
mailed from a bureau drawer in an upstairs room.
They sang a song of themselves, and a fresh wind
carried it. They leapt from a boat or bridge
with a slim volume of suicide notes in hand,
then rose like Lazarus and walked in unseen.
They wrote their names on water, and it flowed.

Cassandra

Because I turned him down, the god Apollo
cursed me with sight. The gift of art is not
the kind you can refuse. No matter what
you do or fail to do, the scenes will follow
you everywhere, assault you in your dreams.
Even if you could turn yourself to wood,
he'd force your hardened fingertips to bud,
and make a garland of your silent screams.
You don't believe me? Though I've heard you sneer
and call me crazy, still you'd have me offer
forecasts of the future. Apropos
of your young daughter, would you like to hear
what day she'll die and everything she'll suffer?
I thought not. No one really wants to know.

Sublimation

If, like amoebas, we could bud,
would beauty pierce us to the heart
and stimulate the rush of blood
that finds release in making art?

The howl of wolves, the song of birds —
those amorous soliloquies —
are kindred to the notes or words
of sonnets and of symphonies.

If we succumb to every urge,
feeding compunction to the flame,
the pathways of our lives converge
on slagheaps of despair and shame.

Yet seize the ferment longing sends,
nor fail to praise Our Lady Lust,
for when her brash dominion ends,
we all will be as chaste as dust.

Farming the Netherlands

Because the frugal Dutch begrudge the sea
each acre it encroaches on the land,
they tie it down with dikes, then pump them free
of water, making polders to expand
their farms. The drowned earth rises, rich with mud,
and sheep and cattle fatten in the field —
until the rare but catastrophic flood
reclaims the land the waters once concealed.

In Amsterdam, in room on windowed room,
tired whores in lingerie sit on display,
listlessly brushing their hair in private gloom
or licking their lacquered lips and beckoning .
to strolling tourists. Why should anything
be free, so long as you can make it pay?

Martial

And then what proper person can be partial
To all those nauseous epigrams of Martial?
                              — Byron, *Don Juan*

Gifted with irony, inclined to mock,
he skewered the pompous rich at all their games,
not hesitant to call a cock a cock,
but cautious when it came to naming names.

He saw the slut inside the prudish matron,
the two-faced skinflint in the man of wealth,
the rotten would-be poet in the patron,
the shabby, grasping suck-up in himself.

He knew that sex and death were democratic,
deflating the pretensions of patricians.
In private, the censorious fanatic
would stoop to some embarrassing positions.

He slept with whores and slave boys, and believed
that pleasure was a service bought and sold,
yet in his tenderest epigrams he grieved
the death of one small slave girl, six years old.

He raised a monument of polished brass,
as permanent as any ode of Horace,
stripping the hypocrites of every class
to tickle, shock, or tweak, but never bore us.

Greek Tragedy

The gods have a peculiar sense of humor.
Their taste in irony is never subtle.
If you dismiss their prophecy as rumor,
they'll kill your wife and child as their rebuttal.

Be wary of the counsel they extend.
They'll warn you of what's coming — in a riddle —
revealing that you'll meet a sticky end,
but leaving out some facts about the middle.

Although it never pays to have them hate you,
it's not much help to have them on your side.
If you are in the right, they'll vindicate you —
usually just after you have died.

Light Verse

The smylere with the knyf under the cloke
— Chaucer, "The Knight's Tale"

Poetry's much possessed by grief.
She contemplates her inner wound,
disconsolate that life is brief
and summer's roses must be pruned.

Light Verse laughs wryly, undismayed,
when praised with dripping condescension.
Privately, she hones her blade
to bring her points to your attention.

Poetry's wisdom lights the page
when not disabled by depression.
Light Verse strikes the match of rage,
consoling through controlled aggression.

Which companion would you choose
to share your bed, to be your wife?
The diva of the daily blues?
The smiler with the hidden knife?

Post-Parting: A Villanizio

Rage, rage against the dying of the light.
Grieve for the memories of delights you've lost;
then light the pyre. Look in your heart and write

of heat his lightest touch used to ignite.
Enlightenment is yours, but at a cost.
Rage, rage against the dying of the light.

No more his mute, adoring satellite,
you won't take lightly being snubbed and bossed.
The light is gone. Look in your heart and write.

He was the lightning; you, poor you, the kite,
alight in one brief, shining holocaust.
Rage, rage against the dying of the light.

Find lighter fluid, matches, dynamite
(it's no light matter, being double-crossed).
Then light the fuse. Look in your heart and write:

call him a lightweight, loser, parasite;
picture him lightly tarred or albatrossed.
Rage, rage against the dying of the light.
Then lighten up: look in your heart and write.

Hedonism

Pursuit of pleasure is its own reward —
and often its own punishment as well.
The epicures of passion soon grow bored
with love, would rather roll a rock in hell
than kiss the same old lips a millionth time.
They're sure that other lips — more piquant, younger —
would stimulate sensations more sublime.
But nothing ever satisfies their hunger.
They worship beauty, can't imagine why
someone gray-haired and wrinkled would excite
desire — chasing their fantasies instead
of looking in the mirror. So they die
still foraging for truffles of delight
when happiness is everywhere, like bread.

Asceticism

Self-denial is the subtlest drug.
It makes you feel related to a saint
to sip herb tea or water, with restraint,
while others gobble chips or chugalug
their beer. The trick is not to seem too smug,
too holier-than-thou, or merely quaint,
but cover with an insincere complaint
about your diet, with a laugh and shrug.

The things you've given up no one can take
away, so every pleasure you refuse
is one less way for loss to make you ache.
You beat death to the cutoff. Still, I choose
to drink the Cabernet, to eat the cake,
to have it all — and lose and lose and lose.

Hypothetical

If I were to kill her, this is how
I'd do it. Late at night, I'd take a knife.
I'd strike as she and Pretty Boy said *Ciao*,
if I were to kill her. This is how
I'd beat the rap, then smile and take a bow,
erasing alimony and a wife.
If I were to kill her, this is how.
I'd do it late at night. I'd take a knife.

Hades in Love

You claim that I had no right to abscond
with your young daughter's slender, blooming body.
Flowers, you know, are rooted in the ground —
she was half mine already.

How could I take her loveliness and youth
to live in Stygian dark, deprived of day,
her peach-bloom cheek corpse-pale, as queen of death?
She knew the price of joy

and you don't — though you wail how much you love her
and want her back in bliss that never fades.
How did I make her stay? What did I give her?
A handful of ruby seeds.

Vanity

On a painting by Frank Cadogan Cowper, 1907

Vanity is such a silly vice.
She drapes herself in velvet and brocade.
Her long blonde hair and rope of pearls cascade
below her waist. She doesn't ask the price
of cutwork oversleeves adorned with braid
or diamonds glinting on her hands and brow,
not stopping to consider when or how
or in what coin the piper must be paid.
At first her upturned chin and downcast eyes
suggest that she's embarrassed to be scanned,
an icon of reserve and modesty —
until, on close inspection, you surmise
she's glancing at the mirror in her hand.

The man I live with thinks she looks like me.

First Snow in October

They do not last, these flakes that fall
before the still-green leaf,
yet they'll return for longer stays,
repeatedly — like grief.

Asylum

It's quiet now in St.-Paul-de-Mausole,
where tourists come to visit Van Gogh's room
and wonder why its peace could not console
his anguished mind. Here irises still bloom;
the hills roll on like waves; the olive trees
shimmer and ripple in the midday sun;
and cypresses point skyward, silent pleas,
like God's own finger or a loaded gun.

But on a dim church wall in that retreat
a scorpion poises, hiding in plain sight,
as still as cast bronze, elegant, infernal —
another refugee. The late-spring heat
made it seek sanctuary from the light,
for scorpions — like nightmares — are nocturnal.

Enemies of the People

Stalin in 1932 decreed
that Soviet art be realist in form
and socialist in content, to be freed
from "formalist" concerns and bourgeois norms.
No landscapes but those changed by human skill
for the people's good; no scenes from private lives;
no portraits but of workers in a mill
or ruddy peasants holding rakes and scythes.
Impressionist smears and dots were disallowed;
paintings that used such tricks, destroyed or hidden
in warehouses. The ones who'd made them, cowed,
conformed or lost their livelihoods. Forbidden
to paint the scenes that shimmered in their sight,
they groaned in private: "But the light, the light!"

Art Appreciation

There's no money in poetry, but then
there's no poetry in money, either.
         — Robert Graves

Money, it's true, prefers the visual arts,
collects on paint and canvas, bronze and stone,
things that appreciate. Money supports
unique and priceless pieces one can own.

Money would rather have its artists dead
than adding artwork to the public store.
An early suicide is guaranteed
to jack up estimation even more.

But poetry is promiscuous, puts out
for anybody who can read or hear,
so poets tend to live from hand to mouth,
who spill their words to any eye or ear.

Poetry is the treasure of despair,
hoarded in sickbeds, gulags, lonely rooms;
invoked to comfort those who need its care;
quoted at funerals and carved on tombs.

Zero-Sum

Your close-knit family, your charming spouse
(your high-school sweetheart, whom you still adore),
your upscale neighborhood and spacious house —
the ones who never win are keeping score.

Your satisfying job, your island cruise,
your trips to France, vacations at the shore —
for everyone who wins, a hundred lose.
The ones who never win are keeping score.

And as your silent tumor starts to grow,
your veins silt up, your glucose levels soar,
your friends will be supportive, but you know
the ones who never win are keeping score.

Study Shows Infidelity Rising Among Seniors

Ah, love, let us be true to one another!
Though waning hormones now can be replaced,
trust, root-pruned, never flourishes in other
gardens. Youth recedes the more it's chased.
Vagifem and Viagra may add drive
to sex lives that have lapsed into routines,
while Botox, lifts, and liposuction strive
to make us as attractive as dead teens,
but only in love's eyes do we possess
the bright hair and trim shapes that once were ours;
only love smiles when hearing us digress
on Tolkien or the Rolling Stones for hours.
None can replace us. You and I alone
can still love one another to the bone.

III. *Like the Boys*

Medea

You might have guessed I wasn't fond of children
back when I carved my brother up. But then,
with Father chasing us, it caused a good
delay. Besides, I wasn't in the mood
to listen to the pampered darling whine
to be sent home. He needed discipline.
And as for your new bride, you might have known
I'd wind up sending her a poisoned gown
rather than plead and grovel in repentance.
You should have seen the little trollop dance
as acid ate her flesh down to the bone.
I gave you all I had and now it's gone.
So take these, too, my final sacrifice
to your ambition, lust, and avarice —
your sons, my bloody masterpiece. They were
the one remaining knot that held me here.
Don't take it as a personal affront.
Some women do what you'd expect. Some don't.

Catullus

What do I see in you, someone inquires,
you brash and cocky playboy, dead at thirty,
and why spend years transcribing your desires?
Your life was loose, your language often dirty.
I doubt I'd even like you, if we met:
you, born to riches, quick to fling abuse,
and loath to waste a thought or epithet
on women you weren't trying to seduce.

But you were from the sticks, thin-skinned, and spurned
by one you ached for, sure she was the one
love of your sorry life. And I have burned
with love, with hate, with words, as you have done,
though now I'm old enough to be your mother.
Hail and farewell, my counterpart, my brother.

Lesbia Replies

Yes, it was fun. And now it's gone.
Give up, Catullus; stop your whining.
Don't keep mooning on and on
about how bright the sun was shining.

Counting kisses just destroys
the mood; I've better things to do.
Go play those games with teenage boys
and I'll find me a man — or two.

My little sparrow's elegy
was sweet (though, frankly, more is less),
but the abuse you've poured on me
won't make me take you back. P.S.,
a married woman hopes to find
a man who *doesn't* speak his mind.

The Monster's Mother

After the monster's death, the monster's mother,
in her impervious carapace of grief,
arrives to pass her loss on to another.

Without her monster, who will ever love her?
It's no use calling him a thug, a thief.
After the monster's death, the monster's mother

knows only that each child is like no other
and only killing others brings relief.
Dying to pass her loss on to another,

she drags one to the bottom to discover
companionship in woe, however brief.
After the monster's death, the monster's mother

clings to despair and fury like a lover.
Guilt comes in waves, pounding her like a reef.
Though she may pass her loss on to another,

the loss remains. Revenge is fleeting. Of her
other desires, oblivion is chief.
After the monster's death, the monster's mother
must die, too. Every loss leads to another.

Easy Money

You get more for your body than your soul,
and even better, you still have it after
they're through with it. It doesn't take much time.
They crack a few bad jokes; you fake some laughter —
the thing is done and you feel no less whole.
What have you lost? Who cares? So where's the crime?
Lie back, say ahh, bend over, and the man
will stuff your piggy bank and pay top dollar.
Try earning that in other jobs. They'd squeeze
each penny. You'd work hard, but live in squalor.
You may as well take them for what you can
when either way they'll have you on your knees.
You hate them all, of course. To them you're just
a walking ashtray where they stub their lust.

Jane Austen

A truth that few would readily acknowledge
is that to know the bleakest facts of life
one needn't go to war, or sea, or college,
or have a baby, or be someone's wife.

Even a girl of modest education
could look around and find it sad and funny
that — brains or beauty, marriage or flirtation —
one's destiny in life came down to money.

Seeing that matches made for love or bread
devolved into indifference or rancor,
she settled for a spinster's life instead,
for time to write and freedom to be franker.

With no man of her own, she still could see
that men, as well, have feelings and frustrations.
Her heroes, men of thought and decency,
mirror her own desires and aspirations.

But though her life was celibate, she knew
of men who were dishonorably intentioned,
of mistresses and bastards, the taboo
subjects that all knew well and no one mentioned.

Her relish for absurdity matched Byron's,
though she was not as rash or histrionic.
She was the opposite of his doomed sirens —
sedate, amused, intelligent, ironic.

She liked his poetry, but didn't care
for Byron's morals or unseemly antics.
Reason and wit they shared, that mismatched pair —
the two great satirists of the Romantics.

Bright Girl

"Bright," like a light bulb, not "intelligent" —
as if the teachers know you're doomed to dim,
fizzling at adolescence as you're bent
into a shape that won't throw shade on *him*.
And if you don't fade out, it's just as though
you had. You'll shine on like a closet light
behind closed doors, or else they'll think your glow
is mere reflection, like the moon's at night.

But why should you cave in to condescension,
a covert thinker, playing dumb and blind,
dodging attack by drawing no attention,
converting slights to irony, resigned
to paradox beyond their comprehension:
your messy house, your origami mind?

Helen

To be the one the lightning singled out
is not a gift — even if you survive.
Men stare, then look away, and women shout
curses behind my back. Dead or alive,
I'm doomed to stir their envy and resentment.
This beauty is a vacuum that destroyed
love, marriage, motherhood, and all contentment,
leaving me floating, airless, in the void
of too much choice and none. If I could change,
I'd rather be a beggar, hideous,
diseased. At least I know how that tale ends.
Instead, through rich halls I drift numbly, strange
and solitary, like Odysseus,
that man of many dodges — and no friends.

Desire

Desire casts out her net, and you forget
the way you thrashed and gasped in it before.
Though you're too old to want to play coquette,
       desire casts out her net
of loss and longing that you can't ignore,
floated by lies and weighted with regret.

Your feet, you think, are firmly on the shore.
You're not a fool, to play Russian roulette
with all you care for, just to feel once more
that mad, electric vertigo. And yet —
       desire casts out her net.

Like the Boys

Dragging on cigarettes, the young girls boast
about how much they drink, how fast they drive,
who's rolled her car more times, who's run the most
red lights, who barely made it out alive
when her car spun out on gravel as she sped
to meet her curfew. One describes with pride
her two-day coma; one, how much she bled
when she wiped out on a motorcycle ride.

So what if their bravado is a bluff.
It works. If you can win your best friends' praise
and end with a bang, who cares about a sequel?
Intent on showing the boys they're just as tough,
they wear their risks like medals. Equal pay's
their mothers' cause. They want to be dead equal.

Emilia to Desdemona

You say you love him. What else can you say
after you've earned your father's curse and fled
to Cyprus? Truth won't keep despair away.
Lie in it if you will, you've made your bed.
You're under marital — and martial — law
now that you've dogged your husband to the wars,
so shut your eyes and ears to every flaw,
for women here are either wives or whores.

You say he loves you. Why then did he rage
at you as if you'd given him the clap?
Men court a goddess and then kick a wife.
Do any foolish thing he asks; assuage
his wrath. It never ends with just a slap.
Next time he'll use his fist. Later, a knife.

Fat Sally's Love Song

A skinny girl's got ice cubes in her soul.
She'll give you half and never give you whole.
But when I eat ice cream, I lick the bowl.

A skinny girl's too needy to stay true.
Her bony hips will poke you black and blue.
Come find out what my featherbed will do.

A skinny girl may look good by your side.
She may buff up the finish on your pride.
But call me when you need to thumb a ride.

A skinny girl will marry you for money
and never laugh at jokes you know are funny.
But you can share my biscuits; pass the honey.

A skinny girl's got black holes in her eyes.
She won't be happy till the day she dies.
If you want loving, try me on for size.

Jane Eyre

Living, as I had, so long in the cold
that one might think my flesh had turned to snow,
often in winter's solitude I strolled
the grounds past dark. That's how I came to know
the master. When his horse slipped and he fell,
I ran to help. He swore at me in rage,
and later, though he hid it, I could tell
his soul paced like a tiger in a cage.

Reader, I married him. I half suspected
that he and madness were already wed.
Each touch, each kiss ended in fire or storm.
But I, who had been taunted, snubbed, neglected
since youth, would rather share a burning bed
than drown in rivers of ice. Rage keeps me warm.

Hazard

The boys who asked you out were never quite
the ones haunting your fantasies at night,
but roses that aren't picked will still turn brown,
and losing is the only game in town.

The ample curves that once were your allure
now give you backaches that you can't endure.
In pain, even your smile looks like a frown,
but losing is the only game in town.

Your grandmother, one friend and then another,
your childhood crush, your father and your mother —
you can't afford it, but you lay them down
when losing is the only game in town.

You hope a few more sunny days are due.
Time answers, "They will come, but not for you."
So "dream," which was a verb, becomes a noun.
Losing is the only game in town.

Delilah

What did he think? That when he swaggered in
after the slaughter, sweaty, rank, and scarlet,
I'd welcome him — the man who'd killed my kin —
with kisses, just another heathen harlot?
I did, of course. One must be wary of
the foaming boar that's crashed into one's room.
I knelt and offered him my abject love,
cast off my robe, dabbed on my myrrh perfume.

His god gave him brute force, muscles of bronze,
a secret, and no sense. Mine gave me rare
green eyes, red lips, breasts whiter than a swan's —
and brains. Besides, I merely cut his hair.
I have my loyalties, as he has his.
Go ask your Judith what the difference is.

Last Words: A Cento

For certain years, for certain months and days,
I measure time by how a body sways.
Everything we look upon is blest;
only we die in earnest — that's no jest.

When sleep comes down to seal the weary eyes
and gathering swallows twitter in the skies,
rage, rage against the dying of the light,
but keep that earlier, wilder image bright.

We shall go mad no doubt and die that way,
with the slow smokeless burning of decay,
the grass below — above the vaulted sky.
Last of all last words spoken is goodbye.

The Author

Susan McLean was born in 1953; grew up in Oxon Hill, Maryland; and received a B.A. from Harvard University and a Ph.D. from Rutgers University, New Brunswick. Since 1988 she has taught English at Southwest Minnesota State University in Marshall, Minnesota. Her poems and translations of poetry have appeared in *The Formalist, Measure, Arion,* and elsewhere. In 2004 she won a McKnight Artist Fellowship/Loft Award in Poetry. In 2006 her poetry chapbook *Holding Patterns* was published by Finishing Line Press.